ELINA EATS

Gluten-Free, Dairy-Free & Paleo Recipes

ELINA CASELL

AuthorHouse™
1663 Liberty Drive
Bloomington, IN 47403
www.authorhouse.com
Phone: 1 (800) 839-8640

Published by AuthorHouse 03/15/2019

ISBN: 978-1-7283-0435-9 (sc)
ISBN: 978-1-7283-0437-3 (hc)
ISBN: 978-1-7283-0436-6 (e)

Library of Congress Control Number: 2019903113

Print information available on the last page.

This book is printed on acid-free paper.

authorHOUSE®

ACKNOWLEDGMENTS

I want to thank Jen Boynton for pushing me to do this book, my parents for always believing in me, and Martha Hill and Hannah Liljekvist, who have helped me turn this idea into reality!

CONTENTS

INTRODUCTION

I grew up in a household in which both my parents were always cooking. Every summer, I spent time with my grandma, who's a great cook and baker. That's where I learned basic cooking skills and developed my appreciation for food.

I've *always* been a foodie, and I love to eat. I have been fortunate enough to travel the world and try some of the best restaurants and foods available, which has built my taste and increased my appreciation for food even more. I love trying different dishes at different restaurants and then trying to copy them, simplify them, and change the ingredients into healthier options without compromising the taste or the experience of the food.

My love for healthy cooking probably started when I had kids. I became more aware of what I put into my body and also what I gave my kids. I've always struggled with stomach pains from different foods, and an allergy test showed that I'm sensitive to both gluten and dairy products. Since then, I've been trying to find alternatives without feeling like I'm on a diet or being restricted, and I've come up with plenty of replacements for the foods I used to cook and love without really compromising the taste or texture. I hope you all will enjoy these recipes and start living a healthier life.

AUTHOR'S NOTE

This book includes imperial and metric measurements. Follow the same unit measurements throughout. Do not mix imperial and metric.

Most of these recipes are made with nut products. If you are allergic to nuts, you should avoid those dishes.

I recommend getting a good blender or food processor to best create some of these dishes. The Vitamix is the best, in my opinion.

As much as possible, try to choose organic ingredients, but it is okay to choose nonorganic produce with thicker skins, such as pineapple, avocado, and watermelon, because the chemicals won't penetrate them as easily.

There is one spice mixture that I use consistently in my cooking. See the recipe for Elina's Seasoning Salt to create your own.

All the recipes in this book are either gluten free, dairy free, vegetarian, vegan, paleo, or all of the above. They are all marked accordingly.

MAIN DISHES

Chicken Lettuce Wraps

CHICKEN LETTUCE WRAPS

NOTE:
Pear-shaped avocados have more meat than round ones because the pit is often smaller. Always leave the pit in the avocado for storage to keep it fresh and from turning brown. You may also put the pit into salads with avocado to keep them fresh.

Ingredients:
1 head butterhead, green-leaf, or romaine lettuce
1 rotisserie chicken, shredded
1/2 red onion, minced
1 avocado
1 handful chopped cashews
1 banana, sliced
Salt to taste

GLUTEN FREE, DAIRY
FREE, PALEO
SERVES 4-6

Break off the lettuce and place on a plate as a taco shell, and then divide the ingredients among the lettuce leaves. Feel free to add dressing, such as aioli, sriracha, or fig-balsamic vinaigrette, or other chopped vegetable or fruits of your choice.

Miso-Glazed Cod

MISO-GLAZED COD WITH CAULIFLOWER-POTATO MASH

Ingredients for cod:

6 cod fillets
1/3 cup low-sodium white or blond miso
2 tablespoon mirin (Japanese cooking wine)
1 tablespoon coconut sugar
1 teaspoon toasted sesame oil
sesame seeds to garnish

For the Cod

Preheat the oven to 375 degrees Fahrenheit. Rinse the fish fillets, and pat dry with paper towels. Combine miso, mirin, coconut sugar, and sesame oil, and stir well until coconut sugar is dissolved. Brush about 2 tablespoons of the glaze onto each fillet. Marinate for at least 30 minutes. Place fish in the oven, and cook for about 5 minutes. Brush with the remaining glaze, and cook for an additional 4–5 minutes. Garnish with sesame seeds.

Ingredients for mash:

1 large head cauliflower
2 potatoes
1 tablespoon dairy-free butter
1/4 cup paleo mayonnaise or coconut cream (optional)
2 teaspoons nutmeg
1/2 teaspoon Himalayan pink salt
1/4 tsp ground white pepper

For the Cauliflower

Cut the cauliflower into florets, and peel and dice the potato. Boil in salted water until soft. Rinse thoroughly, and then blend with the rest of the ingredients until smooth.

GLUTEN FREE, DAIRY FREE, PALEO
SERVES 6

Dairy free sausage stew

SAUSAGE STEW

Ingredients:
1 package gluten-free pasta
coconut oil for frying
1/2 yellow onion, minced
1 package 100 percent beef sausages (not hot dogs)
cream from 1 can of coconut milk
2–3 tablespoons tomato paste
1–2 teaspoons Elina's seasoning salt
almond milk (optional)

GLUTEN FREE, DAIRY FREE
SERVES 4-6

Start by cooking the pasta as instructed.
Sauté the onion in a small amount of coconut oil until golden and soft.
Cut the sausages into 1-inch pieces, and add to the frying pan with the onion. Cook for about 3 minutes.
Add the coconut cream, saving the water for another purpose, and then the tomato paste
and seasoning. If it's too thick, add almond milk or other liquid and stir until all is mixed.

FISH TACOS WITH ASIAN SLAW AND GLUTEN-FREE TORTILLAS

Ingredients:

3/4 cup tapioca flour
3/4 cup coconut flour or rice flour
2 teaspoons garlic powder
1 teaspoon ground white pepper
1 teaspoon sea salt
1 pound white fish such as cod, cut into 1/2-inch pieces
2–3 tablespoons avocado oil

GLUTEN FREE, DAIRY FREE, PALEO
SERVES 3–4

Heat a large pan over medium heat, and preheat the oven to 350 degrees
Fahrenheit. Place a cooling rack over a plate or baking sheet, and set aside.
Mix the flours, garlic powder, white pepper, and salt, and with it coat the fish liberally on all sides.
Once the pan is hot, add the avocado oil. Swirl and heat briefly, and then add some pieces of coated fish
ensuring there is no crowding in the pan, which prevents proper crisping. Do this in two to three batches.
Once the first side is golden-brown and crispy, use a sturdy spatula to
flip to the other side, and brown for a further 4–5 minutes.
When done, place the fish on the cooling rack in the oven to keep warm while the remaining fish cooks.
Serve the crispy fish atop a bed of slaw*; add avocado slices and aioli if desired.

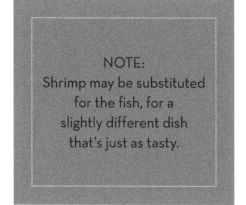

NOTE:
Shrimp may be substituted
for the fish, for a
slightly different dish
that's just as tasty.

*The slaw and tortilla recipes
are found on page 40.

COCONUT CHICKEN WITH BANANA AND SWEET POTATO

Ingredients:
4 chicken fillets
1/2 cup coconut flour
1 tablespoon Elina's Seasoning Salt
1 egg
coconut oil for frying
2 tablespoons shredded coconut (optional)

GLUTEN FREE, DAIRY FREE, PALEO
SERVES 4-6

Wrap the chicken in plastic, and beat with a rolling pin or tenderizer until
flattened and of an even thickness, or cut the fillets in two lengthwise.
In a bowl, mix coconut flour and seasoning salt together.
In another bowl, whisk the egg lightly. Coat each fillet first with
the egg and then dredge in the flour mixture.
Fry in the coconut oil for 3-4 minutes on each side until cooked through.
Serve with banana, sweet potato, side salad, and aioli.

*For sweet potato recipe go to page 37.

Elina's Pasta Bolognese

PASTA BOLOGNESE

Ingredients:
1 1/2 pounds ground beef
cream from 1 can of coconut milk
1/2 yellow onion, grated
2–3 tablespoons tomato paste
Elina's Seasoning Salt to taste
1 teaspoon coconut oil

NOTE:
Keep coconut milk in
the fridge so the cream
hardens and separates
from the water; it will be
easier to remove only
cream from the can.

Start by grating the onion and then put into a nonstick pan with the melted coconut oil. Cook until golden.
Then add the ground beef and sauté until cooked through, making sure to
remove most of the excess fluid and leaving about 2 tablespoons.
Pour in the tomato paste and stir.
Add the coconut milk (only the thick white part; make sure you separate it from the
coconut water because this will determine the creaminess of your meat sauce).
Lastly, add the spice and stir until all is blended well. Serve with gluten-free pasta.

GLUTEN FREE, DAIRY FREE, PALEO
SERVES 4-6

Swedish meatballs with cream sauce and potatoes

SWEDISH MEATBALLS WITH CREAM SAUCE AND POTATOES

Ingredients for meatballs:

1 pound grass-fed ground beef
1/4 cup coconut cream or almond milk
1 egg
1 tablespoon Elina's Seasoning Salt
1 tablespoon olive oil

Ingredients for sauce:

cream from 2 cans coconut milk
1/2 beef Knorr bouillon cube
2 teaspoons Elina's Seasoning Salt
1 teaspoon browning sauce
1 teaspoon brown rice flour (optional)

For the Meatballs

In a large bowl combine the ground beef, coconut cream or almond milk, egg, and seasoning salt, and mix until combined.
Wet your hands with cold water, and form the beef mixture into 1 1/2-inch round meatballs. I prefer them smaller in size.
Heat the oil in a cast-iron skillet on medium heat. Cook the meatballs for about 5–8 minutes per side or until nicely browned on the outside and cooked through.

For the Sauce

Add the coconut cream, saving the water for another purpose, to a small saucepan. Add the bouillon, seasoning salt, and browning sauce, and stir well until the bouillon is dissolved. Add the brown rice flour, if desired, for a thicker consistency.
Serve with boiled potatoes or rice and lingonberries.

GLUTEN FREE, DAIRY FREE
SERVES 4-8

Avocado on Banana-nut Bread

AVOCADO ON BANANA-NUT BREAD

Ingredients:
3 ripe bananas
7 pitted dates, minced
1 cup shredded coconut
1 cup almond flour
1/4 cup gluten-free buckwheat flour
4 organic eggs
3 tablespoons coconut oil
2 teaspoons baking powder
large pinch sea salt
avocado, for serving

GLUTEN FREE, DAIRY FREE,
VEGETARIAN, PALEO
SERVES 5–6

Preheat the oven to 350 degrees Fahrenheit, and line a loaf tin with baking parchment.
Mix the banana and the dates, and then add the shredded coconut, flours, eggs,
coconut oil, baking powder, and salt and mix well with a hand blender.
Pour into the prepared loaf tin, and bake on the middle rack of the oven for 45 minutes.

Serve with avocado and sea salt.

SWEET POTATO GNOCCHI WITH MUSHROOMS AND SPINACH

Ingredients for Sauce:

1 tablespoons olive oil
1 small red onion, minced
2 large garlic cloves, minced
cream from 1 can full-fat coconut milk
1 cup mushrooms, minced and sautéed
1 tablespoon fresh sage, chopped
1 tablespoon tapioca flour (optional)
1 teaspoon salt
1 vegetable Knorr bouillon cube
1 cup fresh spinach

Ingredients for Gnocchi:

1 cup sweet potato, cooked until soft and mashed
1/2 cup cassava flour or tapioca starch
1 teaspoon sea salt
2 tablespoons olive oil

GLUTEN FREE, PALEO, VEGAN
SERVES 4-6

For the Gnocchi

In a bowl stir together the mashed sweet potato, flour, and salt until completely smooth.
Dust a work surface lightly with flour. Divide the dough into four equal parts,
and roll into 3/4-inch-thick logs. Cut the logs into 1-inch pieces.
Bring a large pot of water to the boil, and drop gnocchi into it. Once they have
risen to the surface, remove and drizzle lightly with 1 tablespoon olive oil.
Heat another tablespoon of olive oil in a skillet over medium heat. Add
gnocchi and cook on each side until golden, then remove.

For the Sauce

In a skillet, sauté the minced onion and garlic in 1 tablespoon of olive oil until golden. Set aside.
Add the mushrooms, sage, optional tapioca flour, and salt to the sautéed onion
and garlic. Add the bouillon, and stir until dissolved. Bring sauce to a low boil
and boil for 1-2 minutes, stirring continuously until sauce thickens.
Stir in the spinach, let it wilt, and add the gnocchi. Season to taste.

MUSHROOM SOUP AND STEW BASE

Ingredients:
300 grams mushroom, chopped
1/2 yellow onion, chopped
pinch Himalayan pink salt
cream from 1 can coconut cream
1/2 cup almond milk
1 beef Knorr bouillon cube
1 teaspoon Elina's Seasoning Salt

GLUTEN FREE, DAIRY FREE, PALEO
SERVES 4-6

Add some oil to a frying pan and fry the onions and mushrooms
until golden. Season with Himalayan pink salt.
Place the mushrooms, onions, coconut cream, almond milk, bouillon, and seasoning
salt in a food processor. Process until smooth, and season to taste with salt.

This soup base also works well as a sauce or gravy substitute for any type of
meat or poultry dish. It may also be used to cook a great chicken stew simply
by adding cooked chicken to the stew base and serving with rice.

Baked salmon with cauliflower mash

BAKED SALMON WITH CAULIFLOWER MASH AND CRISPY BRUSSELS SPROUTS

Ingredients:
4 salmon fillets
Himalayan pink salt to taste
lemon pepper to taste

GLUTEN FREE, DAIRY FREE, PALEO
SERVES 4-6

Preheat the oven to 375 degrees Fahrenheit.
Put the salmon on a baking sheet, and season with Himalayan pink salt
and lemon pepper. Bake for 15-20 minutes or until soft pink.
Serve with brussels sprouts and cauliflower mash.

*Find brussel sprouts and cauliflower mash recipe on page 39.

SIDE DISHES

ELINA'S SEASONING SALT

Ingredients:

3 tablespoons salt
1 tablespoon cardamom
1 tablespoon coriander seeds
1 tablespoon chili powder
1 tablespoon garlic powder
1 tablespoon ground black pepper
1 tablespoon ground celery seeds
1 tablespoon ground cloves
1 tablespoon nutmeg
1 tablespoon onion powder
1 tablespoon paprika

Mix all ingredients, and store in a sealed container.

Sweet potato fries

SWEET POTATO FRIES

Ingredients:
3 sweet potatoes
2 tablespoons olive oil
1 tablespoon tapioca flour
1/2 teaspoon garlic powder
1 teaspoon Himalayan pink salt

GLUTEN FREE, VEGAN, PALEO
SERVES 4-6

Preheat the oven to 425 degrees Fahrenheit.
Peel the sweet potatoes; cut them evenly into fries or other preferred shape (e.g., cubes), and place in
a bowl of ice-cold water for at least thirty minutes, which will make them crispier. Drain and pat dry.
Put the sweet potatoes into another bowl, add the olive oil, and toss until
coated. Toss with the tapioca flour and the garlic powder, and mix.
Tapioca flour is not necessary if you chose to cut the potato into chips shape like shown on page 19.
Place on a baking sheet, ensuring the pieces are adequately spaced. Bake for about 15 minutes,
flipping halfway through. Remove from the oven, season, and let cool for about 5 minutes.

KALE CHIPS

Ingredients:
1 bunch kale
1 tablespoon olive oil
1–2 teaspoons Himalayan pink salt

GLUTEN FREE,
VEGAN, PALEO
SERVES 4–5

Preheat the oven to 350 degrees Fahrenheit.
Remove the stems from the kale, and then shred the leaves.
In a bowl, toss the kale with the olive oil and salt until coated.
Spread evenly on a baking sheet, and bake for about 10 minutes or until crisp.

These chips make a healthy snack or side dish.

Brussels Sprout Chips

BRUSSELS SPROUT CHIPS

Ingredients:
brussels sprouts
1 tablespoon olive oil or truffle oil
1 teaspoon sea salt

Cut off the stem of each brussels sprout, and remove the outer leaves. In a bowl, toss with the oil and salt. Place on a baking sheet lined with baking parchment, and bake for approximately 10-15 minutes at 375 degrees Fahrenheit until golden and crisp. These chips are a perfect side dish for meat or just as a snack.

Cauliflower Mash

CAULIFLOWER MASH

Ingredients:
1 head cauliflower
4-5 tablespoons coconut cream
1 garlic clove, minced
1 teaspoon sea salt

Cut the cauliflower into florets, and boil in salted water until soft. Drain. Place in a food processor, and process with the coconut cream and garlic until smooth. Season to taste.

GLUTEN FREE, PALEO, VEGAN
SERVES 4-8

TORTILLAS

Ingredients:

1 1/2 cups almond milk
1 cup bleached almond flour
1 cup tapioca flour
1 teaspoon baking powder
1 tablespoon olive oil or coconut oil

Mix almond milk, flours, and baking powder into a smooth batter, adding a bit more almond milk if it is too thick. Heat a nonstick pan over high with some of the oil, and add 2-3 tablespoons of batter. Fry for about 2 minutes on each side or until done. Repeat until the batter has all been used.

ASIAN SLAW

1/2 small head red cabbage, shredded
1/2 small head white cabbage, shredded
3 large carrots, peeled and grated
1/2 cup unsalted raw cashews
juice of 1 lime
2 tablespoons of agave or honey
2 tablespoons olive oil
1 tablespoon rice vinegar
1 teaspoon toasted sesame oil

Mix all ingredients in a bowl, and serve.

AIOLI

Ingredients:
2/3 cup (100 grams) unsalted raw cashews
1/4 cup plus 2 tablespoons (95 milliliters) water
1 clove of garlic
1 tablespoon lemon juice or apple cider vinegar
1/2 teaspoon salt

Soak the cashews overnight.
The next day, drain and rinse them, and then blend with the rest of the ingredients until smooth. Add more salt if needed.
Store in a sealed container in the fridge for up to four days.

This aioli is a perfect sauce for most dishes, and it works great with chicken, fish, and meat. Why not use it with your sweet potato fries?

GLUTEN FREE, VEGAN

Aioli

GUILT-FREE SWEETS

CHOCOLATE RAW BALLS

Grind the walnuts in a mixer or food processor, and then add the dates, cocoa powder, coconut oil, vanilla extract, and sea salt. Mix until smooth. Form the mixture into small balls, and then roll in the shredded coconut. Rest in fridge for 30 mins.

You can also use this recipe to make a chocolate tart by putting the mixture into a tart pan and chilling. Serve with berries and whipped coconut cream.

Ingredients:
1 1/2 cups walnuts
1 cup pitted dates
1-2 tablespoons raw cocoa powder
1 teaspoon coconut oil
1 teaspoon vanilla extract
large pinch sea salt
shredded coconut to coat

GLUTEN FREE, DAIRY
FREE, PALEO
SERVES 2-4

Banana Pancakes

BANANA PANCAKES

Ingredients:
2 ripe bananas
2 eggs
coconut oil for frying

GLUTEN FREE, DAIRY FREE,
VEGETARIAN, PALEO
SERVES 2-4

Beat the bananas and eggs together until they make a smooth batter.
Heat about 1 teaspoon of coconut oil in a pan, and then pour about 1/4-1/2 cup of batter into the pan. Flip after 2-3 minutes, and cook for a further 2-3 minutes on the other side. Repeat until the batter is gone.
Enjoy with honey and berries.

Raspberry and
lemon sorbet

RASPBERRY-LEMON SORBET

Ingredients:
1 cup frozen raspberries
1/2 cup agave or honey
1/2 cup water
1 tablespoon lemon juice

GLUTEN FREE, DAIRY FREE,
VEGETARIAN AND VEGAN, PALEO
SERVES 6–8

Mix all the ingredients together in a blender or food processor until smooth.
Pour into a loaf tin or other container, and freeze for 30–40 minutes
or until it has reached the desired consistency.
This recipe works great with any other berry of preference.

Fudgy brownie muffins

FUDGY-BROWNIE MUFFINS

Ingredients:

1/2 cup creamy almond butter or cashew butter
1 egg (optional)
3 tablespoons almond flour
2 tablespoons cocoa powder
2 tablespoons coconut sugar
2 tablespoons honey or maple syrup
2 tablespoons unsweetened applesauce
1 tablespoon coconut oil, melted
1 tablespoon unsweetened almond milk
1 teaspoon baking powder
1 teaspoon sea salt
1 teaspoon vanilla extract

GLUTEN FREE, PALEO, VEGAN OR VEGETARIAN
MAKES APPROXIMATELY 10 MUFFINS

Preheat the oven to 350 degrees Fahrenheit.
Mix everything together with a hand mixer, and pour into small-
to-medium-size baking cups. Bake for 10 minutes.
Serve cool, and store in a sealed container to keep them moist.
This is a great mixture for a gluten-free cake bottom as well.